Walks from Kirknewton

By

Peter McEwen

TRAIL GUIDES
publications

First published in Great Britain in 2010 by Trailguides Limited.
www.trailguides.co.uk

ISBN 978-1-905444-35-9

Trailguides Limited
35 Carmel Road South
Darlington
Co Durham DL3 8DQ

Cover design by Steve Gustard

Printed in Great Britain by the MPG Books Group,
Bodmin and King's Lynn

CONTENTS

	Page
INTRODUCTION	
1. The Book	4
2. The Heritage	4
3. Northumberland National Park	7
4. Access and the Right to Roam	8
5. The Walks	9
6. The Weather	10
7. The Maps	11
8. Glendale	12
9. Scheduled Ancient Monuments	12
THE WALKS	
Walk 1 The River Walk	13
Walk 2 Kings and Kilts	19
Walk 3 Yeavering Bell	28
Walk 4 The Tors	34
Walk 5 Hethpool Linn	42
Walk 6 Cheviot Hills Heritage Walk	49
Walk 7 Mid Hill	57
Walk 8 Coldsmouth Hill	65
APPENDIX	
Ferguson Grading System	74
The Author	77
Walking North East	79
Acknowledgements	80
Disclaimer	80
PHOTO GALLERY	81

INTRODUCTION

1. The Book

I first thought about writing a guidebook of walks a few years ago and even went as far as producing three draft walks with maps and text. None of these walks appear in this guidebook but have given ideas for the future. This book is the result of two walks being provided for the Northumberland National Park Cheviot Hills Heritage Project and a chance meeting with Keven Shevels of TRAILGUIDES.

The Cheviot Hills Heritage Project was a two year project which set out to bring together communities on both sides of the Border, in a series of meetings, to celebrate the heritage of the Cheviot Hills and also to construct a Heritage Atlas not only of the history but locations of wildlife, flora and residents' favourite walks. Being a resident of Westnewton I was asked if I would guide two walks as part of Kirknewton's contribution to the project; one walk was to be family friendly and the other to be more strenuous.

The obvious choice for the family walk was the three mile circuit of West Hill and St Gregory's Hill from the village hall. Dorothy Sharp suggested the title "Kings and Kilts at Kirknewton" and so I set out to research the subject. The day of the walk saw me kilted and telling "My-story" to 27 adults, 17 Brownies and their 5 Guiders. I prefer to tell a story when I guide a walk so I always say "My-story" although it is based upon "His-story" or historical research which has come to light after someone else wrote "His-story" (history). The second walk, at the time of writing has not taken place, but is called "Cheviot Hills Heritage Walk" and uses Open Access land to link hill forts and lesser walked hills to the west of Kirknewton.

Keven was introduced to me by Neil Wilson of the Glendale Gateway Trust when I walked into the Cheviot Centre in Wooler one day. Neil explained that Keven was looking for local guides to produce guide books to be added to his stock of publications. Following a brief discussion and subsequent telephone call, I agreed to write a guide book of "Walks from Kirknewton". "Kings and Kilts" is Walk 2 and "the Cheviot Hills Heritage Walk" is Walk 6.

2. The Heritage

Using the format of "My-story" within the walks has led to the general introduction to each walk being given here, so as not to become repetitive. Hopefully this section will be a story in its own right and be informative even if you do not complete all the walks.

Kirknewton was not always called Kirknewton. Originally it was referred to as Newton in Glendale and the church was known as the Church at Newton in Glendale. It was not until 1663 that the two names were combined to Kirknewton meaning the Kirk at the New Town.

Religion has played a large part in the history of Kirknewton and whilst the Church of St Gregory the Great features in Walk 2 "Kings and Kilts", it is possible to visit the Church at the end of any of the walks in this book or even to visit it without doing any of the walks. The History of the Church could be a volume on its own.

We have a long way to go before we reach that point in time – so here is Mystory.

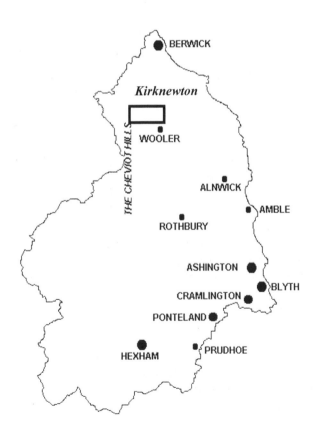

400 million years ago if you had been standing outside the Village Hall at Kirk-newton you would have been standing on the bottom of the sea. 380 million years ago they say there was a volcanic eruption centred to the west of Cheviot which threw the land up to a height of 20,000 feet. 250 million years ago there was an Ice Age and the action of the ice began to take its toll and grind the land-scape down.

We know that man – humanoids – were in Africa 3.2 million years ago because in the 1990's bones were found in Ethiopia by a research team studying sand dunes. The bones turned out to be those of a female who walked upright – dated 3.2 million years ago – named Lucy by the research team as "Lucy in the sky with diamonds" was playing on the radio when they got the bones back to camp. However in 2002 this changed when bones were found in Chad, these bones were those of a humanoid that also walked upright and were dated 7 million years ago. Evidence has also been found to show that humanoids were in Southern Europe 1 million years ago.

In "Britain" the recent discovery of evidence from sea cliffs near Lowestoft has provided a vivid picture of the landscape inhabited by the first "Britains" – a primitive species who used shaped stones as tools 700,000 years ago. Remains found in Boxgrove Quarry in Sussex show that 500,000 years ago big game hunters lived in a climate similar to the present day, but 450,000 years ago eve-rything came to an abrupt end with the spread of a large ice cap, they say 1 mile thick, which came from the north.

400,000 years ago the climate warmed and people came back but disappeared again when the ice returned 380,000 years ago. This cycle of events would re-peat itself about 340,000 and 240,000 years ago and when the ice returned yet again 140,000 years ago the cycle changed, the big game returned but no peo-ple. They say that this is the only time that Britain was without people.

People did return about 60,000 years ago but vanished again 25,000 years ago when yet another ice cap built up. The climate improved 15,000 years ago and people returned again only to disappear again 13,000 years ago when the ice had a final cleansing and it is only in the last 11,500 years that we can talk about our British ancestors living with real continuity.

That last ice age moulded the landscape that you now see around Kirknewton and when it retreated flora and fauna returned and man reappeared. First we had the Hunter Gathers who hunted game, fished and gathered berries etc. They were followed by the Pigmy Flints who used small flint tools and then by the Beaker Folk who had drinking vessels we call beakers. Finally the Celts arrived and brought with them the art of stone hill fort building, examples of which are abundant in the area.

The Tors, the subject of Walk 4.

"My-story" continues in each walk, so put your boots on and walk through this landscape experiencing the history and atmosphere in which the area is steeped.

3. Northumberland National Park

The 60th anniversary of National Parks in England and Wales was celebrated in 2009. It was the National Parks and Access to the Countryside Act 1949 that made provision for the designation of National Parks but we had to wait until 6th April 1956 for the Northumberland National Park to be created, it being the ninth to be officially designated. Covering an area of about 398 square miles (1031 square kilometres) it is one of the remotest and least populated National Parks with only 2000 people living within its boundary. Its symbol is the curlew which can be seen and heard in remote parts of the Park. The Park can be roughly divided into three - farming, forestry and military - which prior to 2000 meant that a large area of the Park had limited access although it was served by rights of way.

National Park Information Centres can be found at Ingram, Rothbury and Once Brewed, all of which offer the visitor a wide range of information and advice including local weather forecasts.

Ingram
Ingram, Powburn, Alnwick, NE66 4LT. Telephone 01665 578 890. Open daily Easter – October.

Rothbury
Church House, Church Street, Rothbury, NE65 7UP. Telephone 01669 620 887. Open daily Easter – October and weekends only November – Easter.

Once Brewed
Once Brewed, Military Road, Bardon Mill, Hexham, NE47 7AN. Telephone 01434 344 396. Open daily Easter – October and weekends only November – Easter.

The National Park maintains an excellent web site where you can find out what's on in the Park, the address is www.northumberlandnationalpark.org.uk.

The National Park also maintains an office in the Cheviot Centre, Padgepool Place, Wooler, NE71 6BL where there is also a very good **Tourist Information Centre** telephone 01668 282 123 which can also provide accommodation information.

4. Access and the Right to Roam

The Countryside and Rights of Way Act (CROW) 2000 was not fully implemented in Northumberland until 28th May, 2005 and even so there are areas where restricted access can still apply until May, 2010. Under the Act walkers and runners are allowed to roam freely on designated "access land" without the need to stay on footpaths or bridleways.

The Act gave all landowners and farmers permission to restrict the "Right to Roam" for up to 28 days per year for management purposes. It also gave two large estates, that of the Duke of Northumberland and Lilburn Estate, the right to restrict freedom to roam with a dog; you can, however, still walk on rights of way with your dog within these restricted areas.

If you wish to know more or find out when and where restrictions apply, visit **www.countrysideaccess.gov.uk**.

The new access land symbol is a circular sign surrounded by a brown ring and containing a brown man standing in a valley with the wording "Access Land". Where dog restrictions apply an additional sign states "Sorry, no dogs - except on rights of way". These signs can be found where rights of way enter Access Land and are usually on gates and stiles. Where a right of way leaves Access

Land you will find the brown man sign with a diagonal strip through him and the words "End of Access Land". Do not be misled by the End of Access Sign – you can still walk on the right of way, but you cannot roam!

The CROW Act does not apply to land north of the Border so that all new Ordnance Survey Explorer Maps show the Access Land coloured light yellow south of the Border and carry the brown man symbol on the cover.

5. The Walks

The walks in this book have been selected to give varied walking ranging from a gentle riverside stroll to the more strenuous hill walks to be found in Glendale, while at the same time experiencing the history and atmosphere in which the area is steeped.

All the walks start and finish at Kirknewton Village Hall, OS Grid Ref NT 913303. Leave Wooler towards Coldstream on the A697 and after three miles turn left onto B6351 (flag poles & Harvey's Restaurant sign) at Akeld, signed Kirknewton, Yetholm. Enter Kirknewton and follow the road as it bends 90 right and then 90 left. Please park outside the Village Hall before the Church in the designated bays or on the new car park in front of the Girl Guides Centre. Please do not park beyond the Girl Guide Centre or the gate to the Church as

Kirknewton Village Hall, the starting point of all the walks.

9

this can affect access for farm vehicles to West Kirknewton Farm.

Kirknewton Village Hall hides two secrets for the visitor/walker. Firstly, it has toilets, which, as part of the funding agreement, are normally open during daylight hours for public use - please respect this facility and leave them as you find them. Secondly, there is in one of the rooms a Museum containing an exhibition entitled "Our Very Own Laura", named after the post lady in the story "Larkrise to Candleford". The museum is only open on certain Sundays during the summer or by special appointment. Details can be obtained from the curator, Dorothy Sharp, telephone 01890 850 285. It should be noted that the external door to the foyer PULLS OUTWARD - serious damage has been done in the past by people trying to push the door to gain entry!

Under normal conditions stout walking shoes would suffice for the riverside walk with walking boots for the remainder. However, following the floods, in wet conditions boots and gaiters would be more appropriate for all walks.

All the walks have way marking in part or in full, ranging from footpath, permissive footpath, bridleway and Hill Fort Trail signs. All of these signs are usually round discs and where they occur on a walk they are mentioned in the text, with key ones listed in the grid reference lists. Specific mention is made in the text where you leave a right of way to utilise your "Right to Roam". See Section 4 - Access and Right to Roam.

The walks should be well within the capabilities of a reasonably fit walker who, on the longer walks, should be equipped for a day in the hills with the possibility of changing weather.

6. The Weather

It will be no surprise to the visitor that the prevailing wind is normally westerly – to corrupt a phase from a well known movie (you have to be of a certain age) – "if the wind's in the west, the trees will lean to the east". The trees in Glendale bend to the east. Kirknewton and Glendale are on the north eastern side of the Cheviots and with the majority of the precipitation being deposited before it reaches the Cheviots we tend to have a drier climate. That does not mean we do not get rain, we do, sometimes more than we would wish – September 2008 saw

5 inches of rain in 36 hours, the devastation of that event can be seen on Walk 1. Normally the driest months are March, April and June and the wettest November, December and January. Strong winds can be a problem on the tops in January, February and March although they can occur at any time as can localised

West Hill seen from the Bowmont Water. West Hill is visited on Walk 2.

bad weather. If you walk all the routes in this book, you may be unlucky and experience a full spectrum of local weather, even in the same day.

Local weather forecasts can be obtained from the Tourist Information Centre in Wooler, telephone 01668 282 123. The Cheviot Centre in Wooler has an open access internet room where for a modest fee you can check the five day forecast from the Met Office.

Unfortunately as mobile phone/wireless internet access is not too good in the area of the walks, except on the tops, you may not be able to use them to obtain weather forecasts. However, if you are on the tops you can look around and see what the weather is doing and what is approaching. Remember to look behind you!

7. The Maps

The Ordnance Survey produces an excellent series of 1: 25,000 scale maps entitled "Explorer". Two sheets cover the area of these walks - sheets OL 16 & 339, although the latter is only needed on Walk 6 and even then only for a couple of miles. If you are purchasing these maps make sure they have the Open Access logo on the cover. The other Ordnance Survey series to consider would be

Landranger at a scale of 1:50,000 with sheet 74 being required. Both of these series of maps can be purchased as All Weather Waterproof Maps and whilst you might consider them to be expensive they do mean you do not need a map case. As an alternative, Harvey's produce a Superwalker weatherproof map "The Cheviot Hills". Personal taste dictates which you choose.

I personally use the Explorer series and if I am walking near the edge of a map I carry the adjoining one which enables me to interpret the terrain to the map and put names to the nearby terrain/hills. It also means that I never walk off the edge of a map and so avoiding becoming misplaced!

The grid references in the walks are given to six figures with their National Grid reference letters. An explanation of the letters and six figure references can be found in the legend printed on all OS maps. It should, however, be noted that a six figure reference refers to the bottom left-hand corner of a square which is 100m by 100m. The references in the walks have been taken from GPS data gathered during the writing of this book, this data was given to 10 figures but as it is impractical to plot to 10 figures on a map they have been rounded up or down to the nearest six figure reference which can easily be plotted on a OS map with the aid of a roamer. Roamers are found around the edges of quality compasses. What this means is that when you plot the reference it may not plot exactly on the named land feature, however by the time you arrive at the plot on the ground the feature should be clearly identifiable.

8. Glendale

The Glen "of the Dale" is mentioned as far back as before 516 and has been the scene of many battles and the baptising of the first Christians – see the walk text for details – and an area of large population.

Visitors today will find a wide range of accommodation including hotels, guest houses, self catering, hostelling or camping and caravan sites, in and around Glendale. To find out where, just visit the Wooler Tourist Information Centre in the Cheviot Centre, 12 Padgepool Place, Wooler, Northumberland, NE71 6BL, telephone 01668 282 123, or any of the National Park Centres previously listed.

9. Scheduled Ancient Monuments

Walks 2, 3, 6, 7 and 8 visit hill forts and it should be noted that as they are Scheduled Ancient Monuments they are protected by law. Please do not disturb the forts and leave as found. Thank you.

WALK 1: THE RIVER WALK

DISTANCE: 3.5 km (2.2 miles)
ASCENT: 42 metres (138 feet)
TERRAIN: Tarmac road and track, field/gravel path
TIME: 1 to 2 hours depending on wildlife seen
START: Kirknewton Village Hall NT 913 303

GRID REFERENCES

Phone Box	NT 915 303
Stile	NT 919 307
Bridge	NT 918 310
Gate	NT 911 307
Joining of the rivers	NT 909 306
Sleeper Bridge	NT 907 306
Road Gate	NT 906 304

FSG GRADING
Grading is T1 (D0, N0, T0, R1, H0)

Distance	0	Up to 6 miles
Navigation	0	No navigation skills needed
Terrain	0	75%+ on graded track or path
Remoteness	1	Countryside in fairly close proximity to habitation – at least 80% of route within 2 miles
Height	0	Less than 100ft per mile

THE WALK

Leave the Village Hall and turn right along the road to the telephone box (NT 915 303) and post box, upon reaching the telephone box turn left down Post Office Lane.

Post Office Lane.

The house on the corner is the Old School House, the former residence of the School Master from the days when the Church School used to be where the Village Hall now is.

The second residence down the lane is Gregory Cottage, where the Post Office used to be, hence Post Office Lane.

There used to be a level crossing where the dismantled railway crossed the lane near the row of three railway cottages. The last crossing keeper still lives in one of the cottages. The story is told that the engine firemen used to shovel coal onto the side of the track when the train went past and that the residents used to collect it in buckets for domestic use.

In September 2008 the River Glen burst its banks here and flowed across the field on the left depositing – they say – 8000 tons of gravel. At the time of writing (July 2009) the farmer is removing the gravel and there are several very large mounds of gravel of different sizes and a temporary hurdle across Post Office Lane (NT 918 306) - carefully undo and then retie the string or step over if it is still there.

Continue along the lane until you reach the stile (NT 919 307) on your left, cross over the stile and proceed across the field to the bridge (NT 918 310). The right of way used to run along side a hedge which was swept away in the flood, so choose the easiest line across the sometimes wet field to the bridge.

Gravel, Bridge and Obelisk.

A second flood in July 2009 and the snow melt of January 2010 flooded the field again and redistributed the mounds of gravel back across the field. As you cross the field, which can sometimes resemble a paddy field, look up to the hill behind the bridge and you will see an obelisk on the skyline. This was erected in about 1827 by Sir William Davison in memory of his father, Alexander Davison of Swarland Park and his brother, John Davison of Lanton.

If you look at the electricity poles you will see that several of them are new. The river swept several away as well and when the cable hit the water it looked like Guy Fawkes Night! The power was off for 36 hours and the flood also took the BT phone line out for seven days.

Cross the bridge over the River Glen, looking out for dippers, grey wagtails, herons, goosanders. and possibly kingfishers. Do not forget to look down, you may see fish. Once across the bridge walk up to the road - this short section can be wet at times. Upon reaching the road turn left and walk along to Lanton Mill.

Take your time walking this section and look over to Kirknewton and the hills behind. The double top hill to the left is Yeavering Bell and as you scan right you see Easter Tor and Wester Tor with St Gregory's Hill, West Hill and The Bell in the foreground. Watch out for butterflies and river birds on this section along with buzzards which frequently circle above the hills to the right of the road.

Approaching Lanton Mill.

Lanton Mill was recently sold and the cottage has been refurbished, the mill, however, is still ruinous. In the 13th century Lanton was part of the Barony of

16

Carham. In 1295 when Baron Ross forfeited his lands it was sold with Kirk-newton to Walter Corbet. Over the years it has had various owners.

Having passed through Lanton Mill, continue straight ahead through the gate next to the finger post "Westnewton ½ Mile" (NT 911 307)

West Newton fingerpost.

As you approach the trees on your left watch out for the joining of the waters (NT 909 306) where the College Burn joins the Bowmont Water from the right to become the Glen.

When you reach the end of the wood on your right go straight on down the slope to the sleeper bridge (NT 907 306). Do not follow the way marker to the right.

The sleeper bridge takes you over the Bowmont Water and you have superb views of Yeavering Bell to your left.

The sleeper bridge.

Continue through the dismantled arch of the railway to the gate at the road (NT 906 304). In front of you is the hamlet of Westnewton and Westnewton House. Go through the gate and turn left to follow the road back to the Village Hall.

As the road crosses the College Burn – in 1556 called Colleche, perhaps from the Anglo Saxon col and leche, a stream flowing through boggy land - at Westnewton Bridge take time to look up and down river for wildlife. Walking back along the road to the Village Hall you pass the Old Station Master's House and the Old Station, part of the Alnwick to Cornhill railway which was opened on 5th September 1887. Catastrophic floods severed the line between Wooler and Alnwick in 1948 and that part closed in 1953. The northern section serving Kirknewton closed to passenger traffic in 1930 but survived for goods until March 1965.

One last point of interest as you pass Catkin Cottage – the gate in the wall is no longer a gate – following the floods of September 2008 the owners took the precaution of having the wall built across behind the gate as a preventative measure.

WALK 2: KINGS AND KILTS

DISTANCE: 5.5 km (3.4 miles)
ASCENT: 199 metres (653 feet}
TERRAIN: Way marked tracks and paths, and a stretch of tarmac
TIME: 2.5 to 3 hours
START: Kirknewton Village Hall NT 913 303

GRID REFERENCES

Old Forge	NT 913 301
Langback	NT 909 298
Way mark	NT 909 291
West Hill Fort	NT 910 295
Stile	NT 912 295
Ladder Stile	NT 915 296
Way mark	NT 916 297
St Gregory's Hill Fort	NT 916 298
Gate	NT 920 301
Road Gate	NT 916 303

FSG GRADING

Grading is F5 (D0,N1,T0,R1,H3)

Distance	0	Up to 6 miles
Navigation	1	Basic navigation skills needed
Terrain	0	75%+ on graded track or path
Remoteness	1	Countryside in fairly close proximity to habitation – at least 80% of route within 2 miles
Height	3	Over 250 ft per mile

THE WALK

Having picked up a copy of the leaflet for the Kirknewton Hill FortTrail from a holder on the wall to right of the display case in the Hall foyer - leave the Village Hall and walk up to and past the gate to the Church, which you will visit on your return. Turn left around the farm buildings and right before the metal gate across the road, following the Hill Fort Trail green way markers. Proceed along the track to the Old Forge (NT 913 301).

Kelly's Trade Directory of 1887 lists three blacksmiths in the area – Kirknewton, Westnewton and Kilham – this is where the Kirknewton blacksmith worked.

Continue past the Old Forge to the ruined cottage of Langback (NT 909 298), which was last occupied in the 1950's, and then to the gate at which you will see the **Access Land** symbol for the first time on the "Walks from Kirknewton".

Entering open access land.

See Introduction Section 4. Access and the Right to Roam.

Go through the gate and continue following the track to the way marker (NT 909 291).
For Walks 3 & 4 turn right at this way marker.

Looking to Wester Tor.

Watch out on this section for deer and wild goats. Ahead of you are excellent views of Easter Tor and Wester Tor.

The parting of the ways.

Leave the way marker and the track by ascending West Hill diagonally to your left, keeping the footpath on your right, to take a line of gradual ascent until you view the small cairn on its summit (NT 910 295). An alternative route is to follow the way marked trail (green Hill Fort Trail discs) shown on the leaflet. I much prefer the diagonal approach allowed by the fact that you are on Open Access Land.

Upon reaching the summit of West Hill take time to explore the Hill Fort. The Hill Forts you see today – West Hill, St Gregory's Hill and Yeavering Bell - are mainly the remains of Celtic Hill Forts. The Celts brought with them the art of stone Hill Fort building, probably on earlier sites which would have had timber palisade fencing on top of an earth mound. The forts on West Hill and St Gregory's Hill have themselves been overlaid with Romano British Settlements and West Hill shows signs on its NE edge of a square Roman Military enclosure. If you look carefully you can still see the remains of hut circles.

Kirknewton from West Hill.

Leave West Hill to the east on a direct line for St Gregory's Hill. At the electric wire fence turn right to the small stile (NT 912 295). Cross the stile – electric fence with rubber cover – and proceed straight ahead following the way markers to the large ladder stile (NT 910 296).

Cross over the stile and go left around the gorse bushes to use the stepping stones across the steam taking care as they can all be slippery and the 7th stone **"wobbles"**! Follow the path uphill to the right around the gorse bushes to the way marker. Keeping the gorse bushes on your left proceed to a second way marker (NT 916 297) which points you to the Hill Fort on St Gregory's Hill (NT 916 298).

Take your time exploring the hill fort and try and find the scooped out floor of the Romano British hut on the NE edge of the fort. The Romans conquered Britain in 43AD with four Legions, but it took them almost 100 years to begin building Hadrian's Wall. When they left in the 5th Century AD, the Saxons swooped down.

23

Above. Ladder stile to stepping stone.
Below. Stepping stones and a kilt.

Retrace your steps to the way marker (NT 916 297) and bear left to go through a way marked gate in the corner of the wall and follow the track, keeping the stone wall on your right, down to the gate (NT 920 301)

As views of the cottages of Old Yeavering come into view, look over the road to the flat grass field behind the Monument at Ad Gefrin. The 200 years between the Romans leaving and the arrival of Paulinus are a little misty, we have no certain knowledge of the affairs of Bernicia – that is what this part of Northumberland was called – we do however have fragments and "KINGS".

Of the 12 great battles in which King Arthur is said to have been engaged prior to 516, the first was probably fought to the east of St Gregory's Hill at the mouth of the Glen. Arthur's chief antagonist in this cycle of battles was Ossa Cylledawr and Ida, who founded Bernicia in 547, was probably his grandson. Ida is said to have had 12 sons – six legitimate and six not so. His six legitimate sons – Glappa, Adda, Ethelric, Theodoric, Frithwulf and Hussa - figured one after the other in uncertain order after Ida died in battle after a 12 year reign. In 600AD Ethelfrid had succeeded his uncle Hussa as King but soon after 617 he fell in battle in Northamptonshire and was succeeded by Edwin.

From 600AD we become aware of a place called "Ad Gefrin" or Yeavering, the place of the goats, where there was a Royal Town.

Nine years after becoming King, Edwin married Ethelburg, a Christian, who was accompanied by Bishop Paulinus who persuaded Edwin to be baptized at York on Easter Day 627. A wholesale conversion of the Northumbrian Nation followed and Paulinus spent 30 days from dawn till dusk baptizing the people in the waters of the Glen just below you.

In 1950 aerial photography showed unusual crop markings in the field across the road from Old Yeavering – a three year long dig disclosed original post holes and the site of a wooded amphitheatre. After you have finished this walk, drive to Old Yeavering, park and follow the way marked trail starting at the Goat Head Gate to the field behind the monument. Interpretive panels tell the story.

Bishop Paulinus was sent by Pope Gregory the Great, the church in Kirknewton bears his name.

Continue the walk following the track down to the gate at the road (NT 916 303). Go through the gate or use the stile, turn left and continue straight ahead through the village of Kirknewton, passing through the metal gate and turning right around the farm buildings to reach the gate to the Church. Take time to

Hut circle, St Gregory's Hill.

visit the Church.

The first mention of the Church is in 1153 when Stephen was alluded to as Parson of The Church at Newton in Glendale. We know that Hugh of St Oswald was vicar in 1285 and Peter Wetewang was vicar in 1293. In 1436 the vicar was given permission to say mass in any safe place within the parish but outside the Church as it was probably in ruins. Excavations in 1857 exposed not only remains of arches of the latter part of the 12th Century but the base of a Norman buttress and foundation but several antiquaries say that the structure possesses evidence of Saxon origin. In 1859 the Architect John Dobson was retained for a complete restoration but this was not carried out in its entirety. The whole nave was pulled down and rebuilt and at a later date an embattled tower was added containing one bell. The nave thus destroyed was substantially a medieval building. During this restoration the sculpture which is now built into the East wall was discovered, some say that it is further evidence of Saxon origin.

The sculpture depicts Lady and Child sitting in a sort of trough which on its right side has a T shaped branch rising from it as though it is meant to be used for tying up cattle. Both have arms raised, the hand of Our Lady seems to be holding something. The Magi are depicted running forward towards them – each carrying a gift in his left hand and his elbow supported on his right hand. They seem to be wearing "KILTS" and have nothing on their feet.

The church of St Gregory the Great.

Leave the Church – remembering to turn off the lights - and return to the village hall, returning the leaflet to the holder.

WALK 3: YEAVERING BELL

DISTANCE: 8.6 km (5.4 miles)
ASCENT: 372 metres (1,221 feet)
TERRAIN: Way marked track and paths, some green, steep descent off Yeavering Bell
TIME: 4 to 5 hours
START: Kirknewton Village Hall NT 913 303

GRID REFERENCES

Old Forge	NT 913 301
Langback	NT 909 298
Way mark	NT 909 291
Gate	NT 913 289
Junction	NT 917 292
Ladder Stile	NT 921 291
Low finger post	NT 923 287
Yeavering Bell	NT 928 293
Way marker	NT 928 294
Gate/stile	NT 924 298
Kings Palace	NT 924 302
Road	NT 924 304
Monument	NT 927 305
Bend	NT 916 302

FSG GRADING
Grading is F6 (D0,N1,T1,R1,H3)

Distance	0	Up to 6 miles
Navigation	1	Basic navigation skills needed
Terrain	1	50 - 75%+ on graded track or path, 25 – 50% off track
Remoteness	1	Countryside in fairly close proximity to habitation – at least 80% of route within 2 miles
Height	3	Over 250 ft per mile

THE WALK

Leave the Village Hall as directed in Walk 2 and continue past the Old Forge and Langback to the way marker at NT 909 291 **at which you turn right for Walk 3.**

Over stream to stile.

Continue to and cross the stream to a stile over the wall, cross over the stile turning left to proceed to a second stile over another wall. Having crossed this stile, proceed diagonally to your right uphill. Initially you will not be able to see your next point of reference but as you proceed uphill another wall with wicket gate (NT 913 289) will come into view. Head for this gate and go through it to join a track at which you turn left.

The track is part of St Cuthbert' Way, which runs from Melrose to Lindisfarne. The route was not walked by St Cuthbert, it links religious buildings with which he had an association.

Torleehouse.

Follow the track past Torleehouse to the way marked junction (NT 917 292)
Torleehouse is so named as it is the house in the lee of the Tors.

Turn right at the junction and follow the track uphill (Green Hill Fort Trail way
markers) through a gate, cross over a stream and continue uphill to a ladder stile
over a wall (NT 921 291)
*Before or after crossing the stile take a rest and look around. Behind you at
the bottom of the track you have just climbed, can be seen to the left West Hill
and to the right St Gregory's Hill (Walk 2) and across the valley Lanton Hill
with its Obelisk (Walk 1)*

Low level fingerpost.

Having crossed the stile continue up hill on the track until you reach a fourway finger post at low level, about a foot above the ground (NT 923 287) **at which you turn left,** (you would go straight ahead for Walk 4). Follow the well defined path downhill to a way marker at which you turn right, continue across the hillside over a small bridge to a stream with no bridge. Cross the stream and start your climb to Yeavering Bell following the well defined green Hill Fort Trail way marked path to the south entrance through the ramparts of the Hill Fort (NT 928 293)

Yeavering Bell with its tumbled stone ramparts is the largest prehistoric hill fort in Northumberland. The wall, thought to have been originally about 10 to 12 feet wide and 7 to 8 feet high and constructed of unhewn blocks – some say originally pink - encircled an area of about 12 acres within which there were at least 130 timber built huts, their sites now marked by slight crescent shaped scoops and platforms. Cadwallader Bates in his History of Northumberland 1895 considers that Yeavering Bell was the Royal Town of Yeavering or Ad Gefrin, but aerial photography in 1950 was to prove otherwise. See Walk 2 "Kings and Kilts"

31

The residents.

Having visited the two tops of Yeavering Bell, return to the low point between the two tops and exit through the tumbled ramparts to the north (NT 928 294) opposite where you entered. Once you have found the first downward way marker the path is way marked at regular intervals as you descend the steep slope to Old Yeavering. Having carefully descended the hill, cross over a stile and proceed down to a gate and stile (NT 924 298). Using the stile in wet weather means you end up in a bog – if it is wet, using the gate gives you drier options. Having negotiated the wet land continue on the way marked path to a gate with stile next to the ruined building. (NT 924 302)

This building, known locally as Kings Palace, is thought to be the remains of a fortified dwelling. In Kelly's Trade Directory 1887, Lee Thomas – rabbit catcher – is listed as living at Kings Palace, Old Yeavering.

Cross over the stile and follow the track past the cottages of Old Yeavering to the road. (NT 924 304). Cross over the road and go through the goat head post gate and walk along the path behind the wall to the site of Ad Gefrin and the Monument (NT 927 305)

Above. Looking west from the cairn on Yeavering Bell.

Do not forget to read the information boards and go through the gate next to the monument to read the plaque from the road.

Retrace your steps behind the wall to the road, turn right and walk back to Kirknewton being aware of the traffic. On approaching Kirknewton go straight ahead through the village, through the metal gate, around the farm buildings past the Church back to the village hall.

As you pass through the village take note of the building with the flat roofed rendered extension on the right, the one with the green door. It was the village reading room, given to the villagers in the 1920's so that the farm laborers could read the newspapers donated by the Estate.

WALK 4: THE TORS

DISTANCE: 17.9 km (11.1 miles)
ASCENT: 664 metres (2,178 feet)
TERRAIN: Way marked tracks and paths, some green. Open access land with less well defined paths.
TIME: 6 to 7 hours
START: Kirknewton Village Hall NT 913 303

GRID REFERENCES

Old Forge	NT 913 301
Langback	NT 909 298
Way mark	NT 909 291
Gate	NT 913 289
Junction	NT 917 292
Ladder Stile	NT 921 291
Low finger post	NT 923 287
Fork	NT 928 281
Road	NT 930 268
Gate	NT 925 266
Fence Corner	NT 922 266
Boundary Stone	NT 916 266
Harelaw Cairn	NT 911 265
Fence	NT 907 267
Hare Law	NT 902 265
Wester Tor	NT 907 272
Low level waymark	NT 916 278
EasterTor	NT 916 281
Ladder Stile	NT 923 287
Junction	NT 917 292
Gate	NT 913 289
Way mark	NT 909 291

FSG GRADING
Grading is F9 (D1,N2,T1,R2,H3)

Distance	1	6 - 12 miles
Navigation	2	Competent navigation skills needed
Terrain	1	50 -75% on graded track or path, 25 – 50% off track
Remoteness	2	Countryside not in close proximity to habitation – less than 20% of the route within 2 miles
Height	3	Over 250 ft per mile

THE WALK

Leave the village Hall as instructed in Walk 3, continue past the Old Forge, Langback, and Torleehouse to the low **level finger post (NT 923 287)**, at which for Walk 3 you would turn left but for **Walk 4 you go straight ahead.** Continue uphill, through a difficult gate – string instead of hinges! – to a way marker at a fork in the track (NT 928 281) at which you keep right.

As you walk along the track look left towards "Tom Tallon's Crag", a large rocky outcrop. Ask who Tom Tallon was and no one seems to know, except that Peter Anderson Graham in his "Highways and Byways in Northumberland 1920" says "Near to it on a hill looking to the Newton Tors stood a large cairn called Tom Tallon's Grave. It was the largest cairn in the district, and on the stones being removed to build a wall, a cist was discovered with bones. The name is supposed to be derived from the Celtic *Tomen,* a tumulus, *Tal,* a forehead or promontory, and *Llan,* an enclosure".

Follow the track as it winds its way across the moor to the tarmac road to Commonburn House. Upon reaching the road (NT 930 268) turn right and continue past Commonburn House. As you leave the buildings behind (on your left) the right of way splits, do not continue straight ahead but aim slightly right across

Commonburn House.

the field to a stile over a fence, cross over the stile and head for the gate in the corner of the field (NT 925 266). Having passed through the gate onto "Open Access" land, (*See Introduction Section 4. Access and the Right to Roam*), leave the Right of Way and bearing right start your climb to Harelaw Cairn on Newton Tors. You are aiming for the corner of a fence (NT 922 266) which is not marked on the 1 – 25,000 map. Upon reaching the corner, keep the fence on your right and continue uphill to another fence at which you turn left. Keeping this fence on your right continue your climb to a Boundary Stone (NT 916 266)

Boundary Stones were used in historical times, before the invention of fences, to mark the boundary either between landowners or parishes. The letters carved upon them denoted landowners or parish initials. This stone is inscribed with a "K" on one side and a "C" on the other. "K" could stand for Kirknewton but the "C"? I will leave the question for you to answer. On the latest edition of the OS map the stone is not on a Parish Boundary although it is within the Kirknewton CP but the next CP marked to the south is Earle. It may therefore be that the stone denotes a landowner boundary between Kirknewton and Commonburn.

Boundary stone.

Whatever it is, as you continue your climb keeping the fence on your right, you come to another Boundary Stone at the bend in the fence.

This Boundary Stone has been uprooted and shows how they were crafted out of a much larger stone before being set in the ground. This one used to have the letter "K" on its exposed face, and I used to consider that it was too heavy to lift to see what the other initial might be. However someone has turned it over because the letter "C" is now exposed. Thinking about it more – they must be landownership stones – perhaps it is "C" for Collingwood who did own the College Valley and Newton Tors (see later on this walk) -in which case what is "K"? On my guided walks I do try and introduce a point of "discussion" with my clients, why not in this book? Suggestions to Trailguides or myself.

As you continue along the fence the ground suddenly steepens and upon cresting the slope Harelaw Cairn (NT 911 265) comes into view on your left. A good spot for an early lunch.

Having visited the cairn, return to the fence and keeping the fence on your right continue uphill past two more uprooted boundary stones to a fence/wall junction (NT 907 267). Go through the gate, turn left and this time keeping the fallen

Above. Uprooted boundary stone.
Below. Harelaw Cairn with The Cheviot in the background.

wall on your left head south west for the large cairn on Harelaw (NT 902 265). Having crossed the sometimes boggy moor, you encounter a slope, at which point you can either follow the wall to its corner and turn right for the cairn or you can aim diagonally right across the slope to the cairn.

Harelaw appears from its name (here, an army, and law, a hill) to have been one of the military stations of the early inhabitants. The large cairn has a very deep recess shelter within it and is another good spot for lunch. Harelaw gives excellent views along the College Valley. To the south is Cheviot itself (815 metres) with the scar of Bizzle Crags directly in front. Bizzle Crags was the scene of the last avalanche fatality in the Cheviots. Beneath the crags is situated Dunsdale, where Sheila the Collie lived during World War 2. Sheila was the only civilian animal to receive the Dickens Medal – the animal equivalent of the VC, which she won for helping to save the lives of an air-crew whose Boeing B-17G Flying Fortress had crashed into Braydon Crags on 16/12/1944. There are many wartime crash sites in the Cheviots, the RAF memorial at the road junction below you in the College Valley and Peter Clark's book "Where the Hills Meet the Sky" give more details.

At the southern end of the valley where the Pennine Way crosses Red Cribs you should be able to make out the last Pennine Way Rescue Shelter, erected with the help of Northumberland National Park Mountain Rescue Team and 202 Squadron RAF Air Sea Rescue from Boulmer. The top to the right of the shelter is The Schil (601 metres)

Leave Harelaw by returning to the wall and retracing your steps across the boggy ground to the wall/fence junction (NT 907 267), where you go through the gate, or use the stile, and go up to the way marked path ahead at which you turn left for Wester Tor (NT 907 272).

Wester Tor gives excellent views down into the northern end of the College Valley and of Hethpool. During medieval times the College Valley was used frequently by Border Reivers and reports of 1342, 1385, 1399 and 1429 claimed that Hethpool had for the most part been devastated by the Scots. 1513, 1541, 1568 and 1596 saw further raids reported – these being the written reports, a lot of complaints would have been verbal.

Roger Grey held Hethpool Tower in 1541 and somewhere along the line the Blackets had ownership. It was because a daughter of Blacket married Admiral Lord Collingwood that a mansion was built. Collingwood was not only famous for the Battle of Trafalgar but for the Collingwood Oaks (Walk 5). In 1919 the mansion was replaced by a more modern mansion in the Scottish style. The Tower ruin is now a feature of the vegetable garden.

Above. Hethpool Linn and the College Burn from Wester Tor.
Below. Yeavering Bell from Easter Tor.

Leave Wester Tor by retracing your steps to the low level way marker previously encountered and keeping left, follow the way marked track to Easter Tor (NT 916 281).

Easter Tor gives excellent views over West Hill and St Gregory's Hill and across to Yeavering Bell (Walks 2 & 3).

From Easter Tor continue to follow the way marked track in a northeast direction towards Yeavering Bell and a ladder stile over a stone wall (NT 923 287). Cross over the stile to the low level finger post which you passed on your outward route. Turn left and follow the track downhill to another ladder stile, cross the stile and continue retracing your steps to the track (NT 917 292) to Torleehouse. Turn left and continue past Torleehouse and having passed the small wood on your right. just before the way marker post look for the wicket gate (NT 913 289) in the stone wall on your right that you passed through previously – watch the step. Proceed diagonally left downhill to cross the two ladder stiles and the stream to the way marker (NT 909 291) at which you keep left to follow the outward track back via Langback and the Old Forge to the Village Hall.

Returning to Torleehouse.

41

WALK 5: HETHPOOL LINN

DISTANCE: 6.5 km (4 miles)
ASCENT: 192 metres (630 feet)
TERRAIN: Way marked tracks and paths, some green and less well defined paths. Short section of path with exposed roots. Some tarmac.
TIME: 2.5 to 3 hours
START: Kirknewton Village Hall NT 913 303

GRID REFERENCES

Old Station	NT 910 304
Finger Post	NT 908 304
Gate	NT 905 296
Stile - roots	NT 904 289
Stile – roots and stones	NT 903 285
Stile	NT 902 285
Bridge	NT 902 284
Way marker	NT 905 284
Gate	NT 913 289
Way mark	NT 909 291
Langback	NT 909 299
Old Forge	NT 913 301

FSG GRADING
Grading is T3 (D0,N1,T0,R1,H1)

Distance	0	Up to 6 miles
Navigation	1	Basic navigation skills needed
Terrain	0	75% + on graded track or path
Remoteness	1	Countryside in fairly close proximity to habitation – at least 80% of the route within 2 miles
Height	1	Over 100 ft per mile

THE WALK

This walk uses part of **Walks 1 & 4** to visit Hethpool Linn and the Collingwood Oaks.

The new stile at Westnewton Bridge.

Leave the Village Hall to the road and turn left to head for Westnewton Bridge passing, on your right, Catkin Cottage, the Old Station and the Station Master's House – all mentioned in **Walk 1.** Immediately **after** crossing the bridge (College Burn) look for the new stile and fingerpost on the left at the end of the stone wall. (NT 908 304)

This is the beginning of the new permissive path to Hethpool and Hethpool Linn. The previous path was eroded in part by the floods of September 2008 and made unsafe. Cross over the stile at the side of the finger post and keeping the fence on your left walk up the field to a ladder stile on your left which you cross over.

Easter Tor and Wester Tor.

Having crossed the ladder stile, proceed with care along the top of the embankment before descending to the sometimes wet valley floor. Keeping the College Burn on your left proceed up stream passing the old ford and the foot bridge that is marked on the OS 1-25,000 map - but does not exist (NT 906 299). Having passed the ford bear right uphill to a gate (NT 905 296) through which you pass to continue uphill to yet another ladder stile/gate.

Cross over the stile and keeping the fence on your right continue to where the fence turns right. From here you go straight ahead on a "not so well defined" path, contouring the hill to reach a stile (NT 904 289) over a fence. Once across the stile the path becomes more defined but does contain the root stumps of previously removed gorse bushes, so please look out for these stumps. You should also be cautious as you walk alongside the fence on your left approaching the next stile (NT 903 285); I have snagged a coat on the top wire which is barbed. Having crossed this stile the path descends to meet another fence which you follow to the next stile (NT 902 285). Once you cross the this stile you descend to the bridge (NT 902 284)

The bridge at Hethpool Linn.

The bridge takes you over the College Burn, but before you cross the bridge walk a little further upstream and, depending on the foliage, you may be able to see Hethpool Linn (waterfall) where the burn narrows through a ravine. Depending upon the time of year it is possible to see fish jumping up the waterfall to reach their spawning grounds higher upstream.

To continue the walk, return to and cross the bridge and follow the path up a sometimes muddy slope and through a sometimes watery meadow! You will reach a way marker (NT 905 284) at which you join St Cuthbert's Way.

St Cuthbert's Way runs from Melrose to Lindisfarne. The route was not walked by St Cuthbert, it links religious buildings and locations with which he had an association.

The goats get everywhere.

Turn left; follow the path down to and across a stream (no bridge) within a wooded dell and up to and over a stile. Continue uphill along the track to the north east towards Torleehouse.

Take the opportunity to look back across to The Bell, the hill to the west of the College Burn around which you contoured. This is where Admiral Collingwood planted lots of Oaks – hence "the Collingwood Oaks". He was most concerned about oak tree conservation, for the fear that the time might come when the building of naval ships would be limited by the lack of suitable oak. His wife looked after the trees when he was at sea, but when he was home and went out walking, he would carry a pocket full of acorns, form a hole with his stick and plant them as he walked. For all his good intentions he did not know that iron would soon replace oak nor that the soil was shallow in his wood, and the trees still there have not matured as he would have wished.

Looking back over Hethpool.

Follow the way marked track uphill, through a wood and over a stile, continuing towards Torleehouse.

Whilst walking this route following the snows of winter 2010, I came across a small whirlpool on the right hand side of the track just before exiting the wood. The melt water had ponded and was draining into the ground with a loud noise and whirlpool effect, if it has been wet keep an eye out for this strange phenomenon.

Upon reaching the next way marker post, look for a wicket gate (NT 913 289) in the wall, approximately 50 feet to your left. Go through the gate – watch the step – and proceed diagonally downhill to the left to a ladder stile over a wall. Cross this stile to a second ladder stile after which you cross to a stream and then proceed to the way marker (NT 910 291) at which you keep left to follow the track around West Hill to the ruined cottage - Langback (NT 909 299) and the Old Forge (NT 913 301) (Walk 2). The track soon turns to tarmac and after you round the corner to the village, turn left at the junction with the metal gate to the right, turn right around the farm buildings to pass the Church on your left and back to the Village Hall.

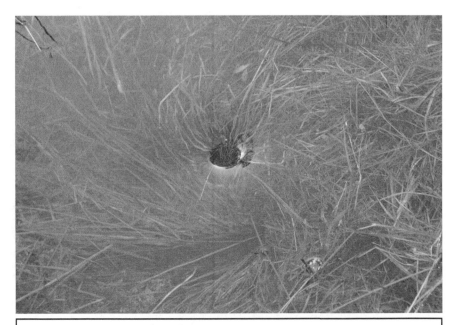

Above. The whirlpool.
Below. The waymarker post.

WALK 6: CHEVIOT HILLS HERITAGE WALK

DISTANCE: 13.2 km (8.2 miles)
ASCENT: 578 metres (1,896 feet)
TERRAIN: Way marked tracks and paths, some green. Open access land with less well defined paths. Some tarmac
TIME: 5.5 to 6 hours
START: Kirknewton Village Hall NT 913 303

GRID REFERENCES

Phone Box	NT 915 303
Stile	NT 919 307
Bridge	NT 918 310
Gate	NT 911 307
Way marker	NT 908 306
Bridge	NT 904 317
Road	NT 898 316
Gate	NT 897 318
Deer Fence Gate	NT 893 318
Kilham Hill	NT 885 311
Gate	NT 883 310
Trig-point	NT 875 302
Gate	NT 875 297
Way marker	NT 881 297
Settlement	NT 882 296
Settlement	NT 884 301
Stile into wood	NT 888 303
Ruin	NT 891 304
Boggy ground	NT 892 304
Into wood	NT 894 303
Wood corner	NT 899 302
Road	NT 903 303
Old Station	NT 910 304

FSG GRADING
Grading is F10 (D1,N2,T2,R2,H3)

Distance	1	6 - 12 miles
Navigation	2	Competent navigation skills needed
Terrain	2	50 -75% on graded track or path, 25 – 50% off track
Remoteness	2	Countryside not in close proximity to habitation – less than 20% of the route within 2 miles
Height	3	Over 250 ft per mile

THE WALK

Leave the Village Hall and follow the directions for Walk 1 as far as Lanton Mill and the gate next to the finger post "Westnewton ½ Mile" (NT 911 307). Go straight ahead through the gate continuing past the river junction as described in Walk 1 to the way marker (NT 907 306) **at which you turn right for this walk,** keeping the trees on your right and the river on your left.

Westnewton House, where you follow the wood around to your right.

The Gurkha Bridge.

As you reach the first gate look left to the dilapidated bridge, this is known locally as the Gurkha Bridge - do not worry you are not going to cross it!

Pass through the gate and follow the overgrown path to the next gate and then to a 3rd gate just before Canno Mill Bridge (NT 904 317). Cross over the bridge and turn right to Canno Mill keeping an eye on the horses that sometimes live in the field. Follow the way markers through the middle of the buildings to emerge on the track at the other side.

The flood of September 2008 swept through all the buildings of Canno Mill, in the front door and out the back – as it were – making the buildings uninhabitable for several months until they dried out. There are still discussions as to why the conversions were allowed to take place without flood defence work being carried out, as locals were aware that the mill had flooded in the past. Three of the properties flooded again during heavy rain in July 2009. In the 13th century Canno Mill was, along with Lanton, part of the Barony of Carham.

Approaching Canno Mill.

Follow the tarmac track uphill over the old railway bridge to the road (NT 898 316) at which you turn right. Being careful of traffic, walk 200m to the way marked metal gate (NT 897 318) set back on the left. At this point you join the way marked Kilham Hill Farm Trail. Go through the gate and head diagonally right uphill on the way marked trail to a gate in a deer fence (NT 893 318) – unmarked on the 1.25000 OS map. Pass through the gate onto "Open Access" land.

(*See Introduction Section 4. Access and the Right to Roam.*)

Follow the way markers through the area of natural woodland regeneration to exit through another gate. The way marked trail continues less well defined to the cairned top of Kilham Hill (338 metres).

Below you to the north is the village of Kilham with its distinctive row of white cottages. Kilham was yet another Carham Barony township, held during its early years by the Archer Family. They sold out in 1353 to John Coupland and like Coupland Estate,Kiham was sold by John's widow to Richard Arundel in 1363. The acquisitive Greys got hold of it in 1408 and kept it until 1913.

Kilham had more than its fair share of raids. There was a pitched battle in

The Deer Gate on the way up Kilham Hill.

1597 which started when four Scots raided one night, broke down a poor man's door and stole all his possessions. His neighbors gave chase and caught three of the Scots but the fourth escaped and raised the alarm and the next day a small army of Scots, some on foot and 40 horse attacked the village. They made no impression as the villagers were waiting and actually took two more prisoners. The Scots then raised 160 horse and foot and descended on the village at 7am. Such a force was unstoppable – all prisoners where rescued, a man slain, seven more terminally wounded and many more were" hurt very sore".

Using your freedom to roam, leave Kilham Hill to the south west to reach a gate (NT 883 310) on the col between Kilham Hill and the next unnamed 327m top. Go through the gate and proceed uphill over the 327m top and then towards the trig-point (NT 875 302) on Longknowe Hill (346m).

Over to your right (NW) in the valley is/was "Antechester". It does not appear on any modern map and its position was not known until documents dating from the reign of Elizabeth 1 were unearthed. These contained reference to a parcel of land "Antechester", SW of Kilham. Although a part of Kilham in

53

16thC, it was separate in its early days – held by William of Akeld as part of the Wooler Barony. In 14[th]C Coupland had it, then it was sold, like Kilham, to Arundel and by him to the Greys. The Greys had little use for such a remote and desolate place – in 1541 it had been described "waste land since before the memories of any man now living". Grey combined it with other purchases to make a larger farm holding and built a farmstead on it. Christopher Dacre's map of 1584 shows a tower, but unfortunately he showed towers that he would like to have seen built as well as those that existed. It would appear, however, that Grey's first farmer tenant was called Thompson and his walls could be his farmstead – Thompson's Walls is shown on the modern map.

Above. Approaching the trig point on Longknowe Hill.

Leave the trig-point by going through the gap in the stone wall and then through the gate in the fence, proceeding south down hill to the gate (NT 875 297) in the corner. You need to pass through the gate – but – be aware of the bog on the other side. Two options – pick your way carefully through it or turn right and keeping the bog on your left walk to a point that you feel safe to cross, cross over and return down the opposite side to the point opposite the gate. Whichever way you decide you now need to head diagonally uphill to southeast on a poorly defined path, passing to the left of a small disused quarry, to level off at a way marker (NT 881 297) on Mid Hill.

100m in front of you (S) (NT 882 296) is the distinctive outline of Mid Hill Fort annotated "Settlement" on the 1.25,000 map. No one has come up with a definite answer as to why Hill Forts exist. It was first thought that they were the protected villages where our ancestors lived as family groups all the time, which may well be how they started out. It would be easier to clear the trees from the tops of the hills to create the Fort than to form a clearing lower down where the view was restricted by dense trees. When our ancestors started clearing larger areas for farming they moved downwards from the hill tops. At this point the Forts are thought to have been used as a place of refuge, safe from attack, and that people lived in settlements lower down. Mid Hill is a possible example of this as it does not have a very defensive position being "overlooked" by other hills.

Return to the way marker and following the green Hill Fort Trail markers proceed northeast to the Fort/Settlement (NT 884 301) on Staw Hill – called Straw Hill on the OS 25,000 map.

Entering the Fort over its distinctive ramparts it becomes apparent that this hill is lower than and overlooked by Mid Hill. It is these two Forts that have given rise to a third theory that in later years as the land become safer they became status symbols, built to show your neighbours how wealthy you were. Staw Hill's south west face is far more impressive that the other sides and

Where you have been, looking back to Kilham Hill.

faces directly towards Mid Hill, it is also lower than Mid Hill so is not defensive.

Follow the way marked trail downhill (northeast) to the way marked stile (NT 888 303) into the wood. Cross over the stile and turning left, walk through the wood until you pick up an easy route to the right and the exit stile. Exit the wood – beware the high bottom step off stile – and keeping the wood on your left walk down hill to the ruined shepherd's cottage (NT 891 304). Do not be tempted to follow the way markers into the wood as the path has not been walked for many years and is too overgrown – in any case it exits the wood 100m further down the hill.

The ruins are all that remains of the original "Staw" which was subsequently replaced with a more modern farm house lower down the valley.

Go through the gate next to the ruin and picking up the way marked path down into the valley, proceed diagonally right down hill to the sometimes muddy valley floor, cross the stream – no bridge – and climb through gorse to the way marked corner of the wood above you. Keeping the wood on your left continue to the stile into the wood (NT 894 303). Cross over the stile into the wood and exit almost immediately via another stile on the other side. Walk east across the field to a gate at the corner of the wood (NT 899 302). Go through the gate and this time keeping the wood on your right continue down hill to a gate at the road. Pass through the gate, turn left and follow the road to a junction amidst buildings. (NT 903 303)

As you approach the junction be aware of traffic coming from your right. The first building on your right – on the inside corner of the bend – is the studio of the artist Peter Podmore. If the door is open, knock and enter, as Peter will be only too pleased to show you his dramatic landscape paintings.

Continue down the road passing the Granary Steps and Westnewton House on your left and then the cottage square of Westnewton on your right. Upon reaching the main road turn right and follow it over Westnewton Bridge to return to the village hall passing the Station Masters House, the Old Station (NT 910 304) and Catkin Cottage on your left as you do so, all mentioned in Walk 1 (The River walk).

WALK 7: MID HILL

DISTANCE: 10.7 km (6.7 miles)
ASCENT: 413 metres (1,355 feet)
TERRAIN: Way marked tracks and paths, some green. Open access land with less well defined paths. Some tarmac
TIME: 4 to 5 hours
START: Kirknewton Village Hall NT 913 303

GRID REFERENCES

Road Junction	NT 905 304
Ford	NT 894 301
Gate	NT 889 298
Way marker	NT 881 297
Settlement	NT 882 296
Settlement	NT 884 301
Quarry – (Disused)	NT 873 292
Wood Corner	NT 876 292
Stile	NT 878 290
Wood Corner	NT 887 289
Fence corner	NT 891 294
Gate	NT 888 297
Ford	NT 894 302
Road Junction	NT 905 304

FSG GRADING

Grading is F8 (D1,N2,T1,R1,H3)

Distance	1	6 - 12 miles
Navigation	2	Competent navigation skills needed
Terrain	1	75% + on graded track or path
Remoteness	1	Countryside in fairly close proximity to habitation – at least 80% of the route within 2 miles
Height	3	Over 250 ft per mile

THE WALK

Passing through Westnewton.

Leave the village hall by returning to the road and turning left to follow the road to its junction (NT 905 304) with the Hethpool road at Westnewton, passing on the way Catkin Cottage, the Old Station and Station Master's House on your right and crossing Westnewton Bridge - see walk 1. Turn left at the junction and passing Westnewton House and the Granary Steps on your right, proceed to the next junction at which the tarmac road turns left, signed Hethpool, and a gravel track leads straight on, finger posted Mid Hill. Following the direction of the finger post, proceed to and through the farm buildings at the Staw – named the Straw on the OS map (this has been corrected on the latest version of the map).

As you reach the Staw your presence will be announced by the barking of several Border Collie sheep dogs. The dogs will not cause you any problems as they are kept in kennel runs behind the buildings.

Above. Looking back to Yeavering Bell from Staw Track.
Below. Yeavering Bell, what a difference the weather makes.

Pass through the gate beyond the farm and follow the track to the ford (NT 894 301), wade through the ford or use the plank bridge to its right and immediately fork left onto a less distinct track, do NOT go through the gate on the track. Keeping the wood on your left follow the less distinct track to where it begins to bend right and rise to a gate. As it begins to rise there is a indistinct path on the left which keeps to the edge of the trees – follow this path to a gate (opposite the end of the wood), undo the string and pass through the gate. Keeping the stream on your left and the gorse bushes on your right, continue to the old dam.

The area between the gate and the dam can be muddy and churned up dependent upon where the cattle have been allowed to roam. The dam itself used to provide the water supply to Westnewton until a few years ago when a new tank was buried in the fields on your right and a whole new system of plastic supply pipe was installed.

From the dam make your way uphill to your right to reach the fence at the top of the slope. Keeping the fence on your right and the trees etc on your left continue to the next gate (NT 889 298). The gate is way marked and there is an Access Land Sign.

See Introduction Section 4. Access and the Right to Roam.

Passing through the gate continue on a well defined grass track uphill to pass through another gate – with stile – to the way marker (NT 881 297) were the track levels off.

At this point – if you are not intending to do walk 6 – you can make a short detour to your right to follow the green Hill FortTrail way markers to Staw Hill hill fort (NT 884 301). Having explored the fort, retrace your steps to the way marker (NT 881 297) and making a short detour proceed to the hill fort/ settlement on Mid Hill 100m away (NT 882 296) – returning again to the way marker (NT 881 297). Both these forts/settlements are detailed in walk 6.

People are often misled at this way marker as there are green Hill Fort Trail way marks together with the yellow bridle way marker, and a well defined green track leading straight ahead uphill. The confusion occurs as walkers misread the yellow way marker and think that it follows the green track uphill – it does not,

Yeavering Bell and Easter Tor as seen from Mid Hill.

it points off to the right. On this occasion, however, you need to be misled as you exercise your **right to roam** and leave the right of way to follow the green track uphill. Follow this track to where it appears to disappear, at this point you bear left to the summit of the hill (352m) and head for the tops of the trees and the small disused quarry (NT 873 292) – an excellent place for lunch.

Looking southwest to the twin cairned top of Coldsmouth Hill (414m) where there are now actually three cairns - Walk 8 - your gaze continues to Town Yetholm and Kirk Yetholm, the finish of the Pennine Way.

Town Yetholm was the residence of the King and Queen of the Gypsies. Stobs Stanes shown on the 1.25,000 (NT 851 280) as Stob Stones, have been used in Gypsy ceremonies and are still used today as part of Kirk Yetholm ceremonies. In the far distance one should be able to see the triple tops of the Eildons, south of Melrose.

Having eaten lunch and/or absorbed the view, to continue walk 7 leave the quarry to the east heading towards the corner of the wood (NT 876 292) where you pick up a green way marked Hill Fort Trail. **However to continue Walk 8 turn to page 66.**

OS maps are very rarely wrong. However, if you are using OS 1:25,000 sheet 16, you will see in the wood an orange permissive path marked – this path does not exist on the ground as shown – it exits the wood at NT 872 291 and skirting the outside of the wood rejoins the marked path at NT 879 288. The path on the ground is way marked.

Follow the way marked path to the timber walk way and stile (NT 878 290) through BlackBog. After crossing the stile head across the hillside keeping an eye open for the difficult to see way mark post on the crest in front of you. Having identified the post, proceed towards it and continue on the way marked path keeping to the crest of the hill through a hill fort – *homestead* - to the corner of the wood (NT 887 289), gate and stile.

Having crossed the fence leave the way marked path, again exercising your Right to Roam, and head for the two standing stones directly in front of you up the slope

These two stones are said to be of Druid origin and to mark the site of a burial mound. Standing between the stones you can just make out the mound you are standing upon.
At the time of writing, I am led to believe that the mound has never been excavated within memory. Some say that it probably never will as Hadrian's Wall was built to stop archaeological research money reaching further north!

Continue up and over White Hill (228m) to pick up a quad bike track towards the corner of a fence (NT 891 294). Keeping the fence on your right continue along the crest to meet a fence joining from the left. Turn left, and keeping this fence on your right continue down hill over rough grass and sometimes wet ground to a wicket gate (NT 888 297) at the bottom of the hill. Go through the gate, cross the stream and turn right to reach a metal gate (NT 889 298).
You passed through this gate on your outward trip and it marks the End of Access Land

Go through this gate and ignoring the next gate immediately on your left, keep the fence on your left to continue along the crest of the slope until you see the old dam on your right. Descend to the dam, then keeping the stream on your right, follow the path to the gate (opposite the end of the wood), undo the string and pass through the gate.

Great Hetha from White Hill.

The area between the dam and the gate can be muddy and churned up de-pendent upon where the cattle have been allowed to roam. It will not have changed since you passed this way earlier in the day!

Keeping the wood on your right, continue to the ford (NT 894 301), wade through the ford or use the plank bridge to its left and continue down the track to the gate at the Staw.

As you reach the Staw your presence will be announced yet again by the bark-ing of several Border Collie sheep dogs.

Pass through the gate and the buildings of the Staw to continue down the track to its junction with the tarmac road from Hethpool, amidst buildings. (NT 903 303)

As you approach the junction be aware of traffic coming from your right. The first building on your right – on the inside corner of the bend – is the studio of the artist Peter Podmore. If the door is open, knock and enter as Peter will be only too pleased to show you his work.

Continue down the road passing the Granary Steps and Westnewton House on your left and then the cottage square of Westnewton on your right. Upon reaching the main road, turn right and follow it over Westnewton Bridge to return to the village hall passing the Station Master's House, the Old Station and Catkin Cottage on your left as you do so, all mentioned in Walk 1 (The River walk).

Leaving Westnewton towards Kirknewton.

WALK 8: COLDSMOUTH HILL

DISTANCE: 19.5 km (12.1 miles)
ASCENT: 875 metres (2,871 feet)
TERRAIN: Way marked tracks and paths, some green. Open access land with less well defined paths. Some tarmac
TIME: 7 to 8 hours
START: Kirknewton Village Hall NT 913 303

GRID REFERENCES

Road Junction	NT 905 304
Ford	NT 894 301
Gate	NT 889 298
Way marker	NT 881 297
Quarry – (Disused)	NT 873 292
Enter wood	NT 872 291
Exit wood	NT 868 291
Ring Chesters	NT 867 289
Gate	NT 863 292
Elsdonburn Shank	NT 862 293
Coldsmouth Hill	NT 857 282
Gate	NT 858 278
Eccles Cairn	NT 855 276
Wideopen Head	NT 861 265
Trowupburn	NT 876 265
Stile	NT 877 269
Great Hetha	NT 886 274
Road	NT 891 274
Stile	NT 896 282
Bridge	NT 902 284
Stile – roots and stone	NT 902 285
Stile – roots	NT 903 285
Stile	NT 904 289
Gate	NT 905 296
Road	NT 907 304
Old Station	NT 910 304

FSG GRADING
Grading is F11 (D2,N2,T2,R2,H3)

Distance	2	12 - 18 miles
Navigation	2	Competent navigation skills needed
Terrain	2	25 - 50% on graded track or path, 50 – 75% off track
Remoteness	2	Countryside not in close proximity to habitation – less than 20% of the route within 2 miles
Height	3	Over 250 ft per mile

THE WALK

Leave the Village Hall and follow the directions for Walk 7 as far as the small disused quarry (NT 873 292). **For walk 8 it might be too early to have lunch at the disused quarry so exit the quarry to southwest to enter the corner of the wood (NT 872 291) via a small wicket gate.** Proceed for a few metres into the wood to pick up the green Hill Fort Trail way mark post at which you turn right and follow the path through the trees to the open area of felling. This area of felling is not shown on the map, so following the defined path through the cleared area, watching out for tree stumps. Continue to the point at which you would have exited the trees (NT 868 291), having skirted around the top of the wood yet to be felled. Go through the gate onto Open Access Land

See Introduction Section 4. Access and the Right to Roam.

Having passed through the gate it is well worth a visit to the Hill Fort of Ring Chesters
(342m) (NT 867 289), so climb the hill directly in front of you or bear right to follow the more gentle climb of the way marked path.

Ring Chesters is a fine example of a ramparted hill fort, the principle being that the gates in each rampart would have been offset so that if your attackers breached the outer gate they would be impeded by your animals that you had

66

Above. Approaching Westnewton.
Below. On route to the ford after The Staw.

herded between the ramparts before reaching the inner gate, giving you more time to rain missiles down on them from the top of the inner rampart. The ramparts would have been of random stone, 10 to 12 feet high and probably the same width.

Elsdonburn Shank and Coldsmouth Hill.

Having explored the Hill Fort proceed downhill to the northwest towards Elsdonburn Shank (NT 862 293) passing through the gate (NT 863 292). Upon reaching the isolated building, go through the way marked gate across the front of the house with its vegetable garden on your right, go through the next gate back onto open access land and turn left. Keeping fences and wood on your left make your way to the summit of Coldsmouth Hill (414 metres) initially via a quad bike track and then free ranging over rough grass. When the bracken is to full height, the quad bike track is difficult to find, so this section of the route can become very strenuous as you make your way as best you can to the summit.

Coldsmouth Hill was/is easily identified by its twin cairns. I say was/is because some one is building a third, which the National Park is planning to remove. From the vantage point of the hill look towards Eccles Cairn - your next port of call – and you may, if the light is right, see the square outlines of a Roman Marching Camp on the north east slope approaching the cairn.

The author on a cold Coldsmouth Hill.

Leave Coldsmouth Hill to the south, to pick up the wood, at which you turn left to reach the wicket gate (NT 858 278) in the fence (50 metres from the wood). Go through the gate, turn right and head for Eccles Cairn (350 meters) (NT 855 276).

As you approach Eccles Cairn you will walk through the Marching Camp – indistinct raised mounds – even if you did not spot it from Coldsmouth Hill.

Eccles Cairn is only 100 metres from the Scottish Border which was defined, some say, by Alexander 11 in 1247 when he agreed to stop raiding into England and keep to his side of the Border. The only problem was that he did not know exactly where the Border was – so he appointed 12 Commissioners to define it. However, some say that it was defined by Alexander 111 in 1257 at the request of his father-in-law Henry 111 (Alexander was married to Henry's daughter) and each appointed three Commissioners for the task. Whichever it was, they both make good stories for a guided walk! When Alexander 111 died after he fell – some say was pushed – off his horse, Edward 1 tried to "dabble" in Scottish politics by trying to marry his son to Alexander's daughter. The Scots were not having any of it and all hell broke out with the Border ceasing to exist as a barrier for the next 400 years – the age of the Border Reiver had arrived.

The Cheviot in the distance with Great Hetha in the foreground.

From Eccles Cairn pick up the well defined St Cuthbert's Way down to the Border Wall. At the Border you have two options – firstly turn left and, keeping the wall on your right, proceed to the next gate, thus staying in England. If, however you feel adventurous you can go through the gate into Scotland, turn left and keeping the wall on your left, proceed to the next gate. Whichever way you choose, at this gate you need to be in England, so if you walked along the wall on the Scottish side, cross back into England now.

The gate marks the crossing of an ancient drove road from Scotland to England – or vice versa – and the secondary fence was erected sometime ago when a period of infection among livestock was in existence – it prevented livestock on either side of the Border coming into contact with each other.

Leaving the wall behind you continue in England following the well defined track past Maddies Well (can be very wet underfoot) to the gate at Wideopen Head (NT 861 265).

Go through the gate to the way mark post and, continuing straight ahead to contour around the hillside on a sometimes eroded track, pass the sheep stell on your left to proceed downhill on a well defined track through gorse to the iso-

70

lated farm of Trowupburn (NT 876 265).

Trowupburn was first mentioned in the reign of King John and has suffered many times at the hands of Border Reivers.

Upon reaching Trowupburn, go through the gate on your left and follow the way marked tarmac track uphill, keeping the buildings on your right, to the next gate. Go through the gate to the finger post; turn right to pass over the stile for your climb to Great Hetha.

The way marked path up Great Hetha has not been in existence long enough to be well defined on the ground, you therefore have two choices – first proceed directly up the hill to the Hill Fort on its summit or follow the meandering quad bike track which does eventually reach the summit (343 metres). I usually start off using the quad track and then about halfway up the hill, take a more direct line.

Great Hetha is yet another Hill Fort which gives excellent views over the surrounding area. If you are using OS 1-25,000 sheet OL16, you will see that it is one of four Hill Forts on the hills protecting the west side of the College Valley - firstly, Little Hetha, then Great Hetha, then Sinkside Hill and finally the un-named 373 metre top. As mentioned in Walk 6 - no one has come up with a definite answer as to why Hill Forts exist. It was first thought that they were the protected villages where our ancestors lived as family groups all the time, which may well be how they started out. It would be easier to clear the trees from the tops of the hills to create the Fort than to form a clearing lower down where the view was restricted by dense trees. When our ancestors started clearing larger areas for farming they moved downwards from the hill tops. At this point the Forts are thought to have been used as a place of refuge, safe from attack, and that they lived in settlements lower down.

Having surveyed the scenery, follow the way marked track off the hill, first north and then northeast down the steep slope to the wall at which you turn right. Keeping the wood on your left follow the way marks down to the road (NT 891 274). Upon reaching the road turn left and follow it to Hethpool (See walk 4).

As you leave the trees behind and you go through the gate with its restriction signs advising Private Road, look out for the large fallen stones in the open grass area at the foot of the slope on your left. These are marked on the OS 1-25,000 map as "Stone Circle" and are the remains of a Druid Stone Circle. The car park you are approaching on your right is the limit of public vehicu-

Leaving Great Hetha.

lar access to the valley. You are free to walk or cycle up the valley from this point but if you want to drive you need a permit – at a cost of £10.00 from Sale and Partners in Wooler who only issue a limited number of permits per day. Permits are not available during lambing which is normally 21st April until 1st June. You are however still able to walk or cycle the valley during this period.

Walk past the car park, over the cattle grid to the way marked cattle grid/gate on your right opposite the cottages. Turn right over the cattle grid (St Cuthbert's Way) and proceed down to the small way marked stile (NT 896 282) over the fence on your left. Cross over the stile – cautious of horses which may be in this field – and cross the field to pass through a small gate in a wall. Once through the gate the way can become wet – a result of the September 2008 flood which devastated the valley and left its mark. Your route ahead goes over the plank bridge to your left – it used to be over the stream but the stream seems to have widened. Once over the plank go uphill and along the ridge on a defined path, with the fence on your left, to reach a stile over a fence.

Once across the stile keep right for another small bridge that used to be over the stream. Make your way as best as you can to keep your feet dry, to exit the damp ground and follow the path keeping the College Burn on your right, to pass Hethpool Linn (waterfall) where at the right time of year you can watch fish jumping their way up stream.

Just before the bridge (NT 902 284), turn left at the way marker for a short sharp uphill climb to a stile (NT 902 285) over a fence which you cross, and keeping the wire fence on you right follow the path through the gorse bushes being very cautious of any root stumps and stones that can be hidden by the grass. The path begins to climb to another stile (NT 903 285). Once across this stile be careful of the barbed wire fence on your right. The path soon leaves the fence and begins to climb to yet another stile (NT 904 289). Cross the stile and continue on a "not so well defined" path to pick up the corner of a fence coming in from your left. Keeping this fence on your left, continue to the ladder stile. Cross the stile and continue on the defined track to the next gate (NT 905 296). Pass through the gate and descend to the valley floor where, keeping the College Burn on your right, follow the path to the old ford and the foot bridge that is marked on the OS 1-25,000 map - but does not exist (NT 906 299).

The bridge which was built by National Park Voluntary Rangers in the early 1980's was a very good bridge. However it was damaged by a flood within two years and whilst at an angle was still usable. Unfortunately the following year another flood finished the bridge off when a tree became stuck underneath it and the diverted water swept the foundations and the bridge away. The most recent floods of 2008 and 2009 have altered the Burn yet again as can be seen by the debris around the ford and have swept away the footpath that used to follow its western bank.

As you follow the burn north away from the ford, look out for the way marker post that now directs you left up a slope away from the burn to a fence along the top of the embankment. Proceed with care along the top of the embankment to the ladder stile, cross over the stile and walk through the field to the new ladder stile at the road (NT 907 304). Crossing over the stile turn right and follow the road over Westnewton Bridge to return to the village hall passing the Station Master's House, the Old Station and Catkin Cottage on your left as you do so, all mentioned in Walk 1 (The River walk)

APPENDIX

Ferguson Grading System (`FGS`)

1. Introduction

The FGS has been adopted as a means of assessing the nature and severity of the various walks in this book and the abilities and equipment needed to tackle each one safely. The FGS was developed by Stuart Ferguson, a long time fell and trail runner, climber, mountaineer, mountain-biker and general outdoor enthusiast. In the opinion of Trailguides the FGS is the most accurate and comprehensive grading system for comparing off-road walking, running and mountain-biking routes anywhere in the country.

2. The System

Tables 1 & 2, set out below, are used in order to give a grading to each route. Table 1 sets out three categories of country that a route could potentially cross, together with a range of factors that would need to be considered when tackling that route. The three categories are, Trail, Fell and Mountain, and after assessing which category best fits the route, a letter, either `T`, `F` or `M`, is allocated to that route. Where a route does not fit perfectly into one of the three categories the closest category is allocated.

Table 2 deals with five specific aspects of the route, distance, navigation, terrain, remoteness and height gain, and each one is allocated a letter, `D`, `N`, `T`, `R`, and `H`. Each letter is also given a severity score from the range 0-3 or 0-4, in respect of distance (`D`). The higher the number, the more severe the route. The five severity scores are then added together to give an overall score. The overall score is then put with the Table 1 category letter (i.e. `T`, `F` or `M`).

In order to show how the grading has been determined for each walk in this book, the five individual severity scores are set out, in square brackets, immediately after the actual grading. So, for example, Walk 4 The Tors has a grading of F9 [D1, N2, T1, R2, H3], indicating that it is a Fell Category walk with a total severity score of 9. This is made up of the five specific severity scores, for distance (`D`), navigation (`N`), terrain (`T`), remoteness (`R`) and height gain (`H`), of 1, 2, 1, 2 and 3 respectively. The highest total severity score which can be achieved is 16 and the lowest total severity score achievable is 0.

The table which accompanies the grading at the end of each walk sets out the specific factors, extracted from Table 2, that need to be considered when tackling that particular walk.

TABLE 1

	TRAIL	FELL	MOUNTAIN
Description	Lowland and forest areas including urban, cultivated and forested locations.	Moorlands and upland areas which may include some upland cultivated and forestry areas plus possibly remote locations.	Upland and mountain areas including remote and isolated locations.
Height	Not usually above 1,000 feet but may go up to 2,500 feet	Usually above 1,000 feet, up to 2,500 feet and above.	Usually above 2,500 feet and up to 4,000 feet.
Way-marking	Usually	Limited	None
Terrain	Usually graded paths, tracks and trails but may include some off-trail	May include some graded paths, tracks and trails but mainly off-trail	Virtually all off-trail
Height gain	Limited height gain	May include considerable height gain	May include some severe height gain.
Effects of weather	Very limited effect	May be prone to sudden weather changes	Extreme weather a possibility
Navigational skills	None to basic	Basic to competent	Competent to expert
Equipment	Walking shoes/boots. Possibly waterproofs Food and drink dependant upon route.	3/4 season walking boots. Full waterproof cover. Possibly map and compass dependant upon route. Food and drink dependant upon route.	Mountain boots. Full waterproof cover. Map and compass. Food and drink
Escape Routes	Yes	Some	Some to nil

TABLE 2

Score	0	1	2	3	4
Distance	Up to 6 miles	6 – 12 miles	12 – 18 miles	18 miles +	24 miles +
Navigation	No navigation skills needed	Basic navigation skills needed	Competent navigation skills needed	Expert navigation skills needed	
Terrain	75% + on graded track or path	50 – 75% on graded track or path 25 – 50% off track	25 -50% on graded track or path 50 – 75% off track	Under 25% on graded track or path Over 75% off track	
Remoteness	Urban	Countryside in fairly close proximity to habitation – at least 80% of the route within 2 miles	Countryside not in close proximity to habitation – less than 20% of the route within 2 miles	Remote, isolated location	
Height gain	Less than 100 ft per mile	Over 100 ft per mile	Over 125 ft per mile	Over 250 ft per mile	

Notes to Table 2

Graded paths = Well established paths with a stable surface.
Escape routes = The opportunity to cut the route short and return to the start without completing the full course in the event of weather changes or unforeseen incidents.

The Author

Peter McEwen

Peter was born and bred in Northumbria and for the past two years has lived part of his life in Westnewton, ten minutes walk from Kirknewton. His interests in maps and navigation began in 1967 when he became a member of Whickham and District Motor Club and could be seen navigating rally cars around the highways and byways of Northumbria. In 1977 he married his wife, Paula, and they became more interested in walking and hill climbing (on foot). Not only have they walked extensively in Northumberland and Scotland, they have also walked in America, Canada, France, Switzerland and Poland.

In the early years of the National Park "What's On" programme, Peter used to back mark for Jimmy Givens – then Head Warden – until one fateful Friday in

1986 when he was asked to guide one of Jimmy's walks as he had been taken ill. 1987 saw Peter guiding his own walks in the National Park Programme, which he is still doing today. In 1989 he became an active call out member of the Northumberland National Park Mountain Rescue Team which he remained with until 2003. He was awarded the Queen's Golden Jubilee Medal for services to Mountain Rescue.

Peter founded **Walk Northumbria** in 2002 and now provides a programme of his own guided walks and guiding for individuals or groups. In his 22 years of leading walks, it is estimated that he has walked in excess of 20,000 miles in Northumberland, during which time he has gained not only knowledge of the hills and countryside, but a vast knowledge of the history and cultural heritage of the area which he uses as narratives on his guided walks.

Peter holds a Mountain Leader Certificate issued by The Scottish Mountain Leader Training Board, undertaking his training and assessment at Glenmore Lodge NOTC, along with a British Red Cross First Aid Certificate and an Enhanced CRB Certificate allowing him to work with children. He is also a member of **Outdoors Northumberland** – the Northumberland outdoors activity provider network.

His hobbies include painting – examples of his watercolours can be see on his web site – photography, cycling and amateur radio which he carries on his walks.

Peter's contact details are:-

Walk Northumbria
Telephone 01668 216 439
Mobile 07764 584 382 – although this does not always have reception.
info@walknorthumbria.co.uk
www.walknorthumbria.co.uk

Walking North East

Walking North East is the brand name for the walking publications produced by Trailguides and reflects the pride that we, as North Easterners, have in our countryside, our history and our culture.

Based in Darlington, we are a small independent publisher specialising in guidebooks centred on the North Eastern counties of England. Our target is to produce guides that are as user-friendly, easy to use and provide as much information as possible and all in an easily readable format. In essence to increase the enjoyment of the user and to showcase the very best of the great North Eastern countryside. Our series of books explores the heritage of us all and lets you see your region with new eyes, these books are written to not just take you on a walk but to investigate, explore and understand the objects, places and history that has shaped not just the countryside but also the people of this corner of England.

If you've enjoyed following the routes in this guide and want news and details of other publications that are being developed under the Walking North East label then look at the company website at **www.trailguides.co.uk**

Comments and, yes, criticisms, are always welcomed especially if you discover a change to a route. Contact us by email through the website or by post at Trailguides Limited, 35 Carmel Road South, Darlington, Co Durham DL3 8DQ.

Other walking books from Walking North East.
At the time of publication the following books are also available but with new titles being regularly added to our publication list keep checking our website.

Northumberland.
The Cheviot Hills.
Kielder Castle.
Walks from Wooler.
The Hills of Upper Coquetdale.
Walks from Kirknewton

County Durham.
Hamsterley Forest.
The Barningham Trail.
Ancient Stones.
The High Hills of Teesdale.
Walks from Stanhope.
Mid-Teesdale Walks.

North Yorkshire.
The Hills of Upper Swaledale.

Walking North East.
Visit our website and sign up to receive our free newsletter, Walking North East, dedicated to walking in North Eastern England. Full of news, views and articles relating to this the forgotten corner of England.

Acknowledgements
Are due to Keven Shevels for the incentive to write the book, to Stu Ferguson for the use of his excellent grading system, to Heather Straughan and Maria and Ian Sharp for test walking and commenting on the routes and to my wife Paula for putting up with unsociable hobbies and pastimes, and for proof reading and correcting the text.

Original ink and watercolours by Peter McEwen.

Above. St Gregory the Great.

Below. Langback. Both from Walk 2 Kings and Kilts.

Original ink and watercolours by Peter McEwen.

Above. The Old Forge - Walk 2 Kings and Kilts.

Below. The Granary Steps - Walk 7 Mid Hill.

Above. The Bowmont in winter.
Below. Yeavering Bell and Easter Tor from Mid Hill.

Above. Towards Canno Mill.
Below. Gnarled trees. Walk 6 Cheviot Hills Heritage Walk.

Above. Canno Mill Bridge. Walk 6 Cheviot Hills Heritage Walk.
Below. Approaching Great Hetha. Walk 8 Coldsmouth Hill.

Above. Great Hetha. Walk 8 Coldsmouth Hill.
Below. The Bowmont Water with Yeavering Bell.

Above. The landscape of walks 6,7 & 8 seen from Yeavering Bell.
Below. Coldsmouth Hill from Longknowe Hill. Walk 6 Cheviot Hills
Heritage Walk.

Above. The Old Station. Walk 1 The River Walk.
Below. Looking west from the cairn on Yeavering Bell..
Walk 3 Yeavering Bell.